LIKE IT IS:
Facts and Feelings About Handicaps From Kids Who Know

LIKE IT IS:

Facts and Feelings About Handicaps From Kids Who Know

By Barbara Adams

Photographs by James Stanfield

WALKER AND COMPANY New York, New York

Library of Congress Cataloging in Publication Data

Adams, Barbara, 1943-
    Like It Is. Facts and Feelings About Handicaps from Kids Who Know

    SUMMARY: A group of handicapped youngsters discuss
their disabilities and how they cope with them on a
day-to-day basis.
    1. Physically handicapped children—United States—
Juvenile literature.   2. Mentally handicapped children—
United States—Juvenile literature.   [1. Physically
handicapped.   2. Mentally handicapped]   I. Stanfield,
James.   II. Title.
HV904.A4   1979   362.4   79-2201
ISBN 0-8027-6374-X
ISBN 0-8027-6375-8 lib. bdg.

First published in the United States of America in 1979 by the Walker
Publishing Company, Inc.

Published simultaneously in Canada by Beaverbooks, Limited, Pickering,
Ontario.

Trade ISBN: 0-8027-6374-X   Reinf. ISBN: 0-8027-6375-8

Library of Congress Catalog Card Number: 79-2201

Printed in the United States of America
10   9   8   7   6   5   4   3   2   1

Book designed by Lena Fong Hor

1943

Contents

This book is dedicated to Danny, Toni, Jed, Sheila and Matt, and to the others, too numerous to mention, who also shared generously their time and themselves.

ACKNOWLEDGMENTS

The author gratefully acknowledges the contribution of the following persons, without whom this project could not have been:

The young people—Danny Frohman; Lita Haido; Jed Rucker; Jon Stevens; Marielle Roloff; Andre Boutillier; Jan Alloway; Perfecto Quesada; Barbara Gieke; Patricia Jones; Matt Ward; Michael Walters; Janine Lorenzine; and Bill Quesnell. The adults—Lydia Radu, M.A.; Allie-Lousie Almore, M.A.; Perry Rosenberg, Ph.D.; Francis Byron, M.A.; Nancy Nesson, M.A.; Karen Lynn, R.N.; and Sandy Bustion, M.A. The schools—William McKinley Junior High, Pasadena, Ca.; Oralingua School, Whittier, Ca.; Lincoln Elementary School, Whittier, Ca.; Marengo Elementary School, South Pasadena, Ca.; Bonita Park Elementary School, Arcadia, Ca.; and Sunset School, West Covina, Ca.

I would also like to express my appreciation to the consultants on the original script: Saul L. Brown, M.D.; Thalians Community Mental Health Center, Family-Child Section, Cedars-Sinai Medical Center, Los Angeles; Etta Fisher and Mary McGinnis, M.A., Oralingua School; Marilyn Graves, Crippled Children's Society, Hollywood, Ca.; Zoltan Gross, Center for Psychotherapy, West Los Angeles; Jack Little, Ph.D.; Kent Wardell, M.A.; Richard Lewis, Ph.D., Cal. State University, Los Angeles; June Taylor, ACSW, Easter Seal Society, Los Angeles; and to Raymond E. Hillis and Mary McGinnis, who critiqued the manuscript and made helpful suggestions.

Special thanks to Jane Stanfield, who was instrumental in the formation of the original concept and whose contribution and suggestions are innumerable throughout.

Barbara Adams
Santa Monica, 1979

Introduction

THIS IS A BOOK about kids and about handicaps. The young people in this book are real people, dealing with actual handicaps and disabilities.

There are many misunderstandings about handicaps. Is a blind person's world totally dark? Are retarded persons weird and unpredictable? Is a learning-disabled child stupid? Does someone with a behavior disorder deliberately cause trouble? Why are we often afraid of the physically disabled? These are just a few of the questions most of us have asked (or wanted to ask) at one time or another.

Just as there are no "typical" individuals, there are no "typical" handicaps. But there are general areas of disability that occur often enough for us to think of them as common. In this respect, most of these young people have common disabilities. The handicaps they live with are not easy, but neither are they strange or extraordinary. A handicap requires a person to make extra effort, or to need extra help in certain ways. A handicap does not necessarily make a person different from others in what he or she feels and needs emotionally. All people need to feel safe, useful, recognized, respected, and loved.

Danny, Toni, Jed, Sheila, Matt, and the other kids on these pages are living successfully in a world that tries to push everyone into the mold of the "normie," that lucky, average person who probably exists only in our imaginations. Yet most of us measure ourselves and others against this fantasy.

Webster's New World Dictionary *defines* handicap as

"... something that hinders one; a disadvantage that makes achievement unusually difficult."

When a person has accepted that disadvantage and learned to deal with it, it is devastating to find that the ultimate handicap is not the disability itself but the reactions of confusion, anger, fear, pity or disgust that it often arouses in others. By sharing the facts about their disabilities, the young people on these pages are saying, "This is what my handicap is. It is less than who I am."

CHAPTER ONE

Hearing and Speech Impairment

Hearing and speech impairments sometimes, though not always, go together. It is easy to understand why a person who cannot hear does not usually speak in a normal manner. People learn to do things by watching and listening to others, then imitating what they see and hear. And they learn more through hearing than through sight. When hearing is distorted or missing, about seventy percent of the information we normally use is lost.

Think about the information that would be missing if you were deaf. How would you learn the word for chair? *How would you ask for, and understand, directions? How would you learn to pronounce words? A person who has a hearing impairment must work extra hard to get the information he or she needs about the environment and to use it effectively in communication.*

Hearing and speech problems are often called communication disorders *because they interfere with the flow of conversation. Persons who have trouble with speech have difficulty letting others know what they think and feel. Misunderstandings can lead to frustration and loneliness. Frequently the person with a communication disorder feels responsible for making other people feel frustrated, annoyed, or confused when they try to communicate. It takes a strong person to keep from being shy or uncomfortable under such circumstances.*

Some speech- and hearing-impaired persons prefer to talk, while others like to use sign language whenever they can because it makes communication faster and easier. It isn't always possible, however, to use sign language since few people know it. Fortunately there are other ways to communicate.

I'm Danny Frohman.

I'm almost thirteen, and I've been playing for the Whittier White Sox for three years. Soccer's a great game. I love working with my team.

It's probably easier for you to read the words I'm saying than to listen to me talk. I'm deaf, and my voice sounds different from what you're used to hearing.

Most of my friends had trouble understanding me at first. A few of them were even a little scared because they thought I was weird. Then the coach explained to them that since I'm deaf, it's hard for me to talk normally. I've never really heard exactly what talking sounds like. I don't have a good example to follow, like I do in soccer.

There are two major reasons why a person's hearing might be impaired. Sometimes an illness, such as rheumatic fever, injures the nerves that carry the sound from the eardrum to the brain. Sometimes the small bones inside the ear are not formed right, so they can't conduct the sound properly. Some people are born deaf, and sometimes the impairment happens later. I was born deaf.

Hearing impairment isn't one exact thing. It can mean not being able to hear anything at all or needing just a little help to make sound louder. It can mean hearing high-pitched sounds but not low ones—or vice versa. A *hearing aid* will help make sound louder. It will also correct for certain kinds of high- or low-pitch losses.

However, even with a hearing aid a person with a severe impairment doesn't hear what *you* hear. The sentence "I don't want to tell my father" might sound like "I told what to tale by water." *Listening training* exercises help me learn to *translate* the sounds I hear into the right words. My hearing aid helps me hear the melody of speech, so that I can tell a question from a statement by the way a person's voice goes up or down, or gets louder or softer.

With the wonderful new hearing aids that are available today, nearly everybody can hear *something*. At some special schools there are classes for tiny babies who have hearing impairments. The infants start to wear hearing aids when they are as young as one month old or as soon as their hearing loss is diagnosed. Their parents and teachers teach them how to listen to the sounds that come through their hearing aids and how to understand what those sounds mean. It looks like they are just playing and having a good time, but all the while they are learning. They also start practicing

DANNY'S HEARING AID

HEARING AID IN POSITION

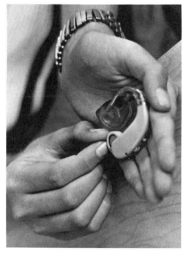

speech right away so that they get used to handling *that* problem and have plenty of time to work with it before they start regular school.

I went to a special school until I was nine. Then I started going to public school, which I like even though it can be hard at times. Besides listening, I have to LOOK at the teacher to get what she's saying. That means I can't goof off as much as I'd like to.

At my old school I learned to talk and to do *speech-reading*—that's what used to be called *lip-reading*. A lot of people think that "reading lips" is as good as hearing but that's wrong. You can't do it across a crowded room like they pretend to do in the movies. In fact, only about one quarter of the speech sounds in English are visible on the lips. The rest have to be figured out from other clues. I have to use both my eyes and my hearing aid. Neither one is enough by itself.

14   Some people try to help me out by talking to me super slow in a really loud voice or by leaving words out of their sentences. They're trying to make it easier, but "YOU . . . WANT . . . GO . . . OUT-SIDE" is even harder to understand than normal speech. It's better if they just speak in their usual manner and make sure I can see their face.

A person may sometimes have to tell me something several times or change the words around a little before I understand. Some words are harder to get than others. It takes patience, but it seems to get easier as we become friends.

Not all persons with hearing problems have speech problems. And not all speech problems are due to hearing impairments. Sometimes speech difficulties are due to the mouth or tongue not being formed correctly, or not working in the usual way. Or nerve damage can mix up the brain's speech centers so that the person knows what he wants to say, but the nerves won't pick up the right words for it. That kind of disorder is called *aphasia*. I've got a little aphasia myself.

Stuttering is a very common speech problem. Most experts on speech think that everybody stutters a little when they first learn to

talk. Then if too much attention is given to the stuttering, the person gets anxious and stutters even more. Family and friends should help a stutterer by listening without making comments or trying to assist.

There are many different reasons why a person might need *speech therapy*. Some kids go every day, and some go only once or twice a week. The speech therapist helps them to correct their mistakes and to learn better sentence structure and pronunciation.

A speech therapist is a little like a coach, and speech therapy is like practice. You know how outfield chatter makes a batter nervous? It's a kind of teasing to try to prevent a good hit. In the same way, teasing a person who has a speech problem makes it harder for that person to talk well. But that kind of teasing is not part of a game. It should *never* be done.

I probably won't ever speak perfectly, though I'll get better than I am now. I have speech therapy every day with Ms. McGinnis. She's nice and she's pretty, but she makes me work hard. First we check my hearing aid to be sure the battery is working properly. Then she starts a lesson. I have to listen to every word, and if it's something new or something I have trouble with, I carefully watch her lips, tongue, and throat to see how the word is formed.

I feel her chest and cheek to get the right sound vibrations. Then I repeat the word or sound after her. There are lots of drills. It can get really boring.

When people with hearing problems can't get enough information from sound and from speech-reading, they might learn to spell out words with their fingers or make special signs for words with their hands. In *finger-spelling,* each position of the fingers represents a letter of the alphabet. In *signing,* each position of the hand usually represents a complete word. Sometimes it represents a whole sentence—sort of like a code, or like the hand signals we use in a ball game.

DANNY WORKS EVERY
DAY WITH THE
SPEECH THERAPIST,
MS. McGINNIS, TO
IMPROVE HIS
COMMUNICATION
ABILITIES.

17

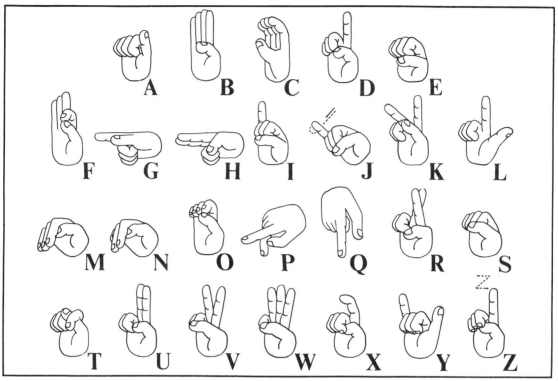

The finger-spelling alphabet is always the same, but there are several different languages in sign. I speak a little of the one called *Ameslan*. Anyone can learn to sign- or finger-spell. It's fun, especially when you want to talk without somebody else finding out what you're saying.

Some hearing-impaired persons prefer to use only sign- or finger-spelling and not use their voice at all. I don't feel that way because there would be too many people I couldn't talk to then.

I figure that if things go the way I want, I can't limit myself just to people who sign. I've got plans for high school, playing soccer and baseball, and then college or professional sports, if I'm good enough.

Being deaf sometimes makes me mad. It doesn't seem fair that I have to work so hard at communication. But that's how it is, and I'd still rather be me than anyone else I know.

CHAPTER TWO

Visual Impairment

One person in every four needs his or her vision corrected in some way with glasses or contact lenses. One person in every three thousand is legally blind. Of those who are legally blind, only a very small number are unable to see anything at all.

Many people think that blindness is the worst disability to have. Because they really enjoy seeing beautiful sights, watching television, and noticing the appearance of friends and strangers, they find it difficult to imagine life without those things. Seeing makes people feel safer, too. Although a visual impairment can be very inconvenient, it seldom cuts down as much on the information a person receives from the environment as a severe hearing impairment does.

Some people have the idea that a blind or visually impaired person has a "sixth sense" about things. That is not true. A visually impaired person simply learns to make greater use of the sensory clues in the environment. He or she learns to listen more carefully and feel more acutely because that extra information helps make up for the lack of sight. It's a matter of paying closer attention to things that a sighted person ignores or skips over lightly. Additional attention to something may mean additional enjoyment received from it.

My name is Toni—

Antoinette, really, but I'm called Toni. The *other* reason they asked me to be in this book is because I have so many hobbies. I like rock music, especially, and dancing and reading historical novels. And I have lots of pets—two dogs, a rabbit, two hamsters, and a couple of turtles. They took quite a few pictures of me and my "menagerie."

Maybe you can't tell from the pictures, but if we met in person you'd probably notice right away that I'm blind. You'd know by my cane, and by my eyes. With other kids like me, it's sometimes even more obvious.

I know many people feel funny about meeting a blind person. I remember the time my friend Leslie introduced Linda and me to David. Poor David! He was really nervous. That's probably the

THE BLINDNESS IN THESE CHILDREN IS MORE OBVIOUS THAN IN TONI.

worst thing about having a handicap—the way it affects other people's reaction to you. I didn't notice it so much when I was younger, but when I started junior high, I noticed it a lot.

I'm in the eighth grade now, and I've been going to classes in a regular junior high for the past three years. At first it was really scary being with regular kids because I'd been at a school where all the kids had problems like mine. But after everybody got used to me and I got used to them, I started to love regular school. Having friends who understand makes all the difference in the world. It makes you feel free.

My old school was a special school for blind kids (we usually use the more modern term *visually handicapped* or *VH*). That's where I had my *mobility training*, which I'll tell you about later, and where I learned *Braille*. Braille is a system of writing that uses raised dots, like bumps, on the paper. I read by feeling the bumps. I write by typing them on a machine called a *Braillewriter*. I can also use a regular typewriter.

I still go back to my old school for extra help and for special events. The last time I was there was for the Pantera Rally. Every

22

TONI'S CLASSROOM   A BRAILLEWRITER

year the members of the Southern California Pantera Club set up a
sports car rally especially for the school. Each member drives his or
her own car, while the navigator is a VH kid who's navigating from
Braille directions. The directions are tricky, such as, "Three miles
west to the inventor of the steam engine, then left two blocks to the
father of our country."

Some of my sighted friends were surprised that VH kids could
be navigators in a rally, or that we would want to participate. When
people first see a group of kids like those at my old school, they

TONI WITH
ONE OF THE
OFFICIALS
BEFORE THE
PANTERA

23

usually think of helplessness and of being totally in the dark. But it's not like that. For one thing, we're *not* helpless. For another, very few of us are "totally in the dark." There are different kinds of visual handicaps and different degrees of blindness.

The law says that a person is *legally blind* if he or she has 20:200 vision or less in the better eye while using all possible help, such as glasses or contact lenses. That means the person can *see* something from twenty feet away that a normally sighted person can see from two hundred feet. However, the legally blind person probably won't see it clearly. And often he or she can only see things that are *very* close.

Bill, who is legally blind, might see light-colored shadows and outlines.

What Sally sees is more like what you see when it's dark.

Sometimes a person sees only the center part of what others see. That's called *tunnel vision*.

Losing sight in the *center* is a symptom of *glaucoma,* the most common eye disease.

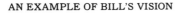
AN EXAMPLE OF BILL'S VISION

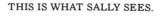
THIS IS WHAT SALLY SEES.

SEEN BY A PERSON WITH TUNNEL VISION   HOW A PERSON WITH GLAUCOMA SEES

THE CAT IN FOREGROUND, SEEN BY A FARSIGHTED PERSON, IS OUT OF FOCUS, WHILE THE PLANT, FARTHER AWAY, IS IN CLEAR FOCUS.

A NEARSIGHTED PERSON SEES THE NEARBY CAT DISTINCTLY, BUT THE PLANT IN THE BACKGROUND IS BLURRED.

Nearsightedness and *farsightedness* are usually less serious problems and easy to correct with glasses or contacts. A *far*sighted person sees *distant* things clearly, like the plant in the pot. But something close, like the cat, is blurred. *Near*sightedness is just the opposite. The cat is easy to see, but the plant looks fuzzy.

"Totally blind" probably sounds terrible to a seeing person, but it isn't. I was born without sight, so I don't miss it as much as you might think I would. Without sight there are still music and sounds, friends to talk to, fragrances, and how things feel when you touch them. There's thinking and daydreaming, physical activities, and all the various emotions. It's a full life. With so much going on, I

don't have time to be very sad about something I haven't ever experienced.

Most kids with visual problems were born with them. We're used to being the way we are. What's bad is when people feel so sorry for us that we start to feel sorry for ourselves. Sometimes it's hard to avoid thinking of yourself the way others think of you. It's especially hard when we get left out of things because someone believes we can't understand what's happening.

With special training even a totally blind person can do quite a lot. When I walk down the street, I swing my white cane along the ground in front of me to find out if there is anything in my way. I also listen carefully for clues that give me information, such as traffic noises and familiar sounds.

Learning to get around is called *orientation and mobility training*. Instead of canes, some people have dog guides. However, you must still know how to get where you're going whenever you go to a new place. The dog doesn't *take* you there. It just lets you know where walls and doors and obstacles are located, much like the cane does.

In learning mobility, you start by feeling. You protect yourself from bumping into things by holding your arms in front of your body. One arm protects your chest and face; the other, your stomach and thighs. This method of travel is called *trailing*. It's mostly for little kids.

When you get older, you learn to use the cane or a dog. You memorize where many things are, especially at home and at school and at other important places. It requires concentration and paying

TONI'S CANE ALERTS HER TO A CURB.   TONI DEMONSTRATES *TRAILING*.

attention all the time. Maybe that's one reason kids sometimes think I'm so serious—because I'm concentrating.

Once in a while, somebody comes along and asks if I want help crossing the street. I appreciate their thoughtfulness. Of course, like anyone else, I have to be careful about strangers. When I'm crossing the street with a person, or walking with a friend in an unfamiliar place, I like to use the standard method that all VH people use. I hold his or her arm just above the elbow. In a tight space, the person moves the arm behind her and I automatically walk behind. I can follow really well that way, and it's a nice way to travel.

I love to go to the shopping center, but buying clothes can be a problem. Since I can't tell what color something is, my friends help me pick out my clothes. When I get home, I make Braille labels for things that feel similar but are different colors, such as jeans and T-shirts. With the labels to tell me the colors, I can get dressed without asking for help.

Other aids that people with visual handicaps use in learning, working, and playing include books with large print, hand-held magnifiers, TV-screen magnifiers, special systems and rules in games and sports, talking computers, and records and tapes.

There are records called *talking books* because they contain the reading of an entire book but speeded up to go faster than normal speech. I know how to listen very quickly!

The high school I'm going to next year is a regular high school. It has a room with all the special equipment I might need to keep up with my schoolwork, such as textbooks in Braille and on tape, and a teacher to help and advise me. I'll go there when I need to between my regular classes.

There's one thing I still want to know more about and I hope my friends will help me, because it's important and I can't learn it by myself. It's how to come off okay around other people—you know, how to be popular and "in" on things. I suppose everybody spends some time trying to figure that out. Handicapped kids, though, might need extra help. For instance, VH kids sometimes forget to hold their heads up. Sometimes they're ashamed of how their eyes look. Well, they have to get over that. A friend can remind them to look up by saying, "I'm over here. Look at me." A severely VH person like me has to be told who and where you are, especially if you approach unexpectedly. Often it's hard to tell who someone is by their voice alone.

By the way, don't be afraid to use words like "look" or "see" around me or any other VH person. It doesn't embarrass us. In fact, it's embarrassing when people try to avoid those words, because it can't be done. Besides, we have a good idea of what those words mean. We use them, too.

29

I like to be treated the same as everybody else, so far as possible, and that's pretty far! I've found that I can do more things than most people think I can. Maybe not everyone with a visual handicap gets around as much as I do. Most of them could, though, if they had the chance to learn and to practice. I bet they *want* to. I know *I* want to. Because I like people. I like the world. And I think it's going to like me!

CHAPTER THREE

Orthopedic Handicaps

There are many different kinds of orthopedic handicaps. What they all have in common is a physical condition that makes it difficult or impossible for the person to move his or her body in the normal way. If you had a broken arm or leg, you would be temporarily orthopedically handicapped. Most orthopedic handicaps, however, are more permanent.

Common physical problems affecting movement include cerebral palsy, paralysis, amputation, various diseases of the nerves, muscles, and bones, and brain damage.

The words "handicap" and "disability" cause a lot of confusion in a subtle way. This is because people often take those words as meaning more than they actually do. For instance, a person who must use a wheelchair is referred to as "handicapped," but what does that really mean? He or she might still go to college, play certain sports, hold a job, get married and raise a family, and do many other things. The <u>amount of inconvenience</u> that the disability causes is the handicap the person experiences in doing those things. The person is handicapped in doing them, but not necessarily unable to do them.

How much a person is handicapped depends upon the special problems and personal talents of the particular individual, as well as on changes that can be made in his or her surroundings. Often, the environment can be changed in ways that decrease or eliminate the inconvenience of a disability. For example, a ramp instead of stairs makes it possible for a person in a wheelchair to enter a building. Special hand controls allow him or her to drive a car.

I'm Jed.

I've got Legg-Perthes Disease. I got it two years ago, when I was six. It's a disease that affects the top of the thigh bone (femur) and the hip joint. The braces take pressure off the bones so they can heal properly. In a few years I'll be able to walk normally again, and I won't need the braces anymore.

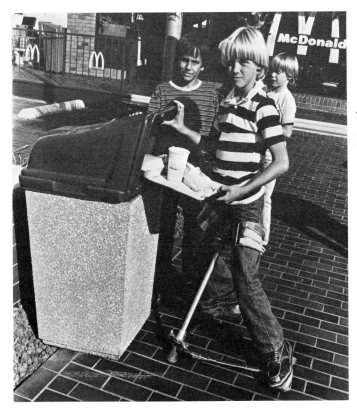

JED'S BRACES MINIMIZE PRESSURE ON HIS HIPS AND THIGH BONES.

I'm glad about that. Wearing braces can be a drag, especially when they keep you from doing something fun. Or when people look at you funny or are afraid of you. I don't like that, but I understand why it happens. When I first saw my friend Jon, I never thought *I* would be friends with him. And Marielle, who's got cerebral palsy—she walks and talks like a broken puppet.

Those kids were scary to me at first. I guess I thought that because they looked different on the outside, they might be strange on the inside. But once I got to know them, all that changed.

The word *handicap* means something that hinders you, something that gets in your way sometimes, so that you do things a bit differently to get around it. An *orthopedic handicap* means that some part of your body can't move in the usual way.

There are many different kinds of orthopedic problems, some more severe than others. Often, the person is born with the problem. But it can also occur because of an accident or an illness. One thing for sure, neither the orthopedic problem nor the illness that caused it is *catching*. In fact, about the only things that are really catching are colds and measles.

When I first met Jon, I had the weird feeling that if I hung around with him, maybe my legs would get worse and I'd become like he is. I didn't know where I got that feeling. You see, I already had my braces, and I knew I wasn't going to have to wear them all my life. I also knew I couldn't catch what Jon had from being with him. So why did I feel like that?

My Dad explained that everybody has a primitive part of his or her brain that sometimes has illogical thoughts that aren't true in reality. These thoughts can give a person some strange feelings. My Dad said that whenever I have uncomfortable feelings that don't make sense, I should talk them over with him. And he suggested that I try to get to know Jon a little better.

Well, I became friends with Jon, and he's a neat guy. I don't

MARIELLE WALKS BY HERSELF.

JAN DEPENDS ON HIS
WHEELCHAIR FOR
LOCOMOTION.

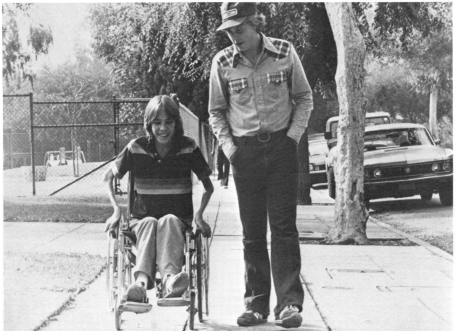

have any of the feelings I started out with now that I know him.

Jon had an illness called *peroneal muscular atrophy*, which injured the nerves that carry the signals from his brain to his legs. When nerves are damaged, the signals are not passed along to the muscles, so the muscles don't move. They are *paralyzed*. A paralyzed muscle doesn't grow or develop. That's why Jon's legs are thin and small.

Jon used to go to a school for handicapped kids only. One day he invited me to a special sports meet there. By that time I knew him pretty well and I was curious, so I went. It turned out to be really interesting! There were kids who had come from all over the state to compete. The games and contests were set up so that a person's disability didn't make any difference. Kids in wheelchairs were racing each other, competing in archery and shot put, and playing basketball on teams. There were obstacle relays for kids in braces and with crutches. Some of those kids could do fantastic things. I got very excited when Jon almost took first place in his race. It was a real athletic game, just like any sports contest. That

THESE KIDS DON'T LET HANDICAPS KEEP THEM FROM COMPETING.

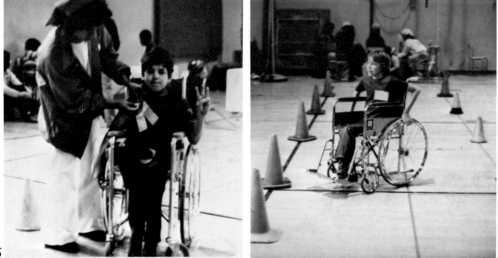

THIS YOUNGSTER ON CRUTCHES
TAKES PART IN A RELAY.

JED TALKS OVER HIS PAPER
WITH HIS TEACHER.

was something I didn't expect.

I'd never seen anything like that school before. I always went to regular school. When I got my braces, they just changed a few rules so that I could stay right along with my class. I'm still on most of the teams I used to be on. When we play baseball, I bat and someone runs for me. Of course, I can't do *everything*. But there are lots of things I can do.

After Jon's race, a real cute girl came over to congratulate him on his second-place medal. She was in a wheelchair like Jon, but she seemed to have trouble talking, as if she couldn't make her mouth work quite right. That's how I met Marielle.

Marielle has cerebral palsy. When she was born, something injured the part of her brain that controls the movement of her muscles. Her brain sends her muscles signals to bend, even when Marielle doesn't want them to. Because of that, her movements are shaky and jerky. Her speech is hard to understand because the muscles in her jaw are affected. It takes a lot of effort for Marielle to walk and talk and move the way *she* wants to. It's a good thing cerebral palsy isn't painful. It's sure inconvenient, though.

37

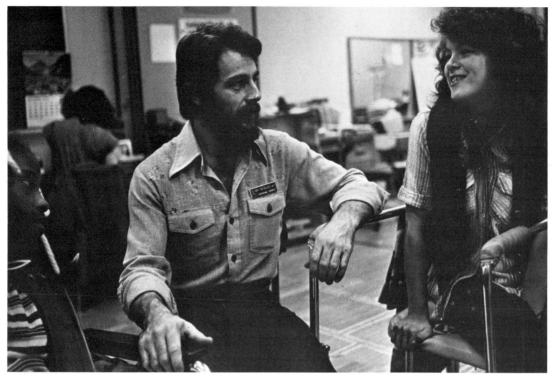

Marielle spends part of every day in *physical therapy*. She does special exercises that help her muscles to relax and to grow stronger. It can be hard work.

Another kind of orthopedic handicap happens when you lose a part of your body, like an arm or a leg. I don't think I would call Andre "handicapped," however. Nothing stops *him* from anything!

Andre lost the bottom part of his leg, just below the knee, after a bicycle accident. Andre himself helped make the decision to have the leg amputated when it became necessary. Now he has an artificial leg made of rubber and plastic.

An artificial body part is called a *prosthesis.* Andre's been using prostheses since he was five years old. As he gets bigger, he gets new ones that fit his new size. His prosthesis doesn't do any fancy tricks like the Bionic Man, but he can do just about anything else.

38

ANDRE LETS A FRIEND EXAMINE HIS PROSTHESIS AND SHOWS HIM HOW IT WORKS.

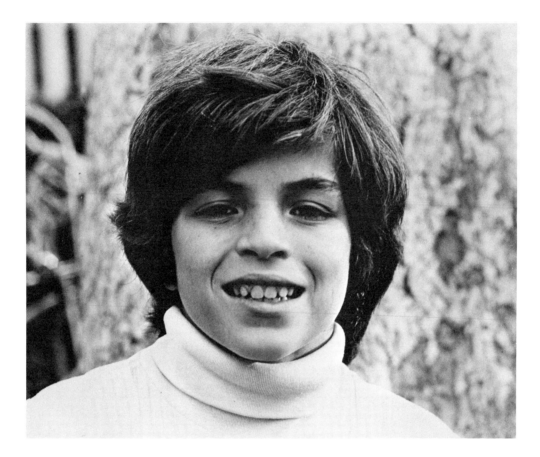

Sometimes he turns the foot around and walks into class backwards!

Many people use a prosthetic arm or leg after they lose their own through an accident or illness. Others decide not to use one if they think they don't need it. It can be hard getting used to not having a part of your body. Some people feel ashamed of themselves at first. Why should they? They're still the same *inside* as they used to be. After all, when it comes to what you like in a person, that's what's most important.

Most people who meet Andre don't even know he has a prosthesis. But he doesn't mind showing them if they ask about it.

Once a guy at McDonald's asked me about my braces, I was

glad. When he understood he didn't think it was anything weird. Maybe he guessed that it's better to politely ask about a person's disability than to keep silent and come to the wrong conclusion.

KIDS WITH HANDICAPS PREFER POLITE QUESTIONS ABOUT THEIR PROBLEMS TO BLAND INDIFFERENCE.

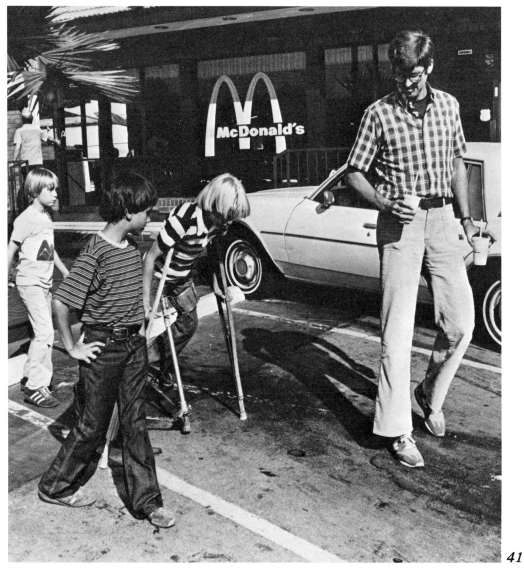

Maybe he knew that I'm just myself—Jed—and I've got a certain kind of problem that I've got to deal with. I just happen to talk a little better than I walk. It could have been the other way around. So what!

CHAPTER FOUR
Developmental Disabilities/ Mental Retardation

Developmental disabilities interfere with one's ability to perform life tasks by limiting physical and/or mental responses. Not all developmental disabilities include the problem of mental retardation, but that is what people often mean when they use the term "developmental disability." The major developmental disabilities are cerebral palsy, mental retardation, epilepsy, and autism.

About fifty to seventy-five percent of all persons who have cerebral palsy experience some degree of mental retardation. Epilepsy and autism are not usually accompanied by retardation.

A mentally retarded person will need a longer period of time to learn something than the average person. Frequently, more difficult things will not be learned at all unless they can be broken down into small, simple steps that are taught one at a time.

The degree to which a person can be mentally retarded varies quite a bit. There are three major classifications: 1. mildly retarded (EMR)*; 2. moderately retarded (TMR)*; 3. severely or profoundly retarded (PMR)*. About eighty-five percent of all retarded persons are mildly retarded. With extra help and special classes, most of them can complete high school and become employed.

A moderately retarded person usually completes the lower grades, plus training that enables him or her to handle everyday living and, perhaps, to be employed in a sheltered work setting.

Severely retarded persons usually require special care, but new teaching methods and discoveries are now making it possible for them to learn more than it had been thought they could.

*See Glossary

Hi! I'm Sheila.

I'm here to explain some things about kids who are developmentally disabled. I know a lot about that.

I have *one* kind of developmental disability. Some people call me *mentally retarded* because it takes me longer to learn things than it takes most people.

Often, with new information, I won't understand right away. I might need things explained more slowly and in a more simple way than usual. But once I get something, I don't forget it.

For example, if you tell me your telephone number, it'll take me longer to memorize it than it took you, but once I know it, I'll

SHEILA CONCENTRATES IN CLASS.

remember it as long as you will. When I don't have time to memorize, I write things down.

Certain things, such as word problems, I don't get at all. A problem like this:

> *Mary has twice as many oranges as Tom, and Tom has one third as many as Bob. If Bob has two-and-a-half dozen oranges, how many does Mary have?*

I can't handle! Of course that doesn't mean I couldn't memorize the price of oranges and sell them in a store. I could, and so can most of the people who are called *retarded*.

I hate the word "retarded" because it makes some people think I'm out of it, or crazy—a kind of monster with weird ideas. Or they think I can't be trusted. That's unfair because it's just not true. Still, *that word* gives a lot of people bad feelings. And it gives them the wrong idea about many nice kids. I wish they would get rid of it!

I spend most of my school time in a regular eighth-grade class. At my school they don't say, "Sheila is retarded." They say, "Sheila needs extra help." They help me when I need it. The rest of the time they treat me like everybody else.

There are other kids at my school with developmental disabilities. Some of them don't go to regular classes, but they have recess and assembly with the rest of the school.

Janie and Bill are two kids who spend all day in Ms. Bingham's special education class. Ms. Bingham teaches reading, writing, and *ADL,* which stands for "Activities Of Daily Living." That includes such things as making change, traveling on buses, and personal grooming. Most kids learn those things easily without even noticing it. But kids like Janie and Bill need extra help and practice with ADL, besides extra help with their school work.

JANIE   BILL

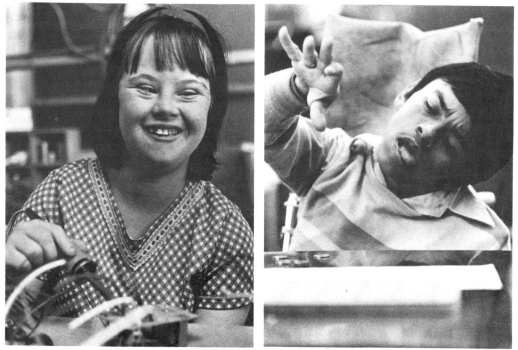

Janie has *Down Syndrome*. Down Syndrome isn't catching—you have to be born with it. It's the result of having an extra chromosome in the cells. The doctors know *how* it happens but not *why*. It could happen to anyone.

Janie is seventeen years old, although she looks and acts younger. She can read and write about as well as a third grader. Some Down Syndrome kids read and write quite well, and others have a hard time. I don't think it matters too much, as long as they have the chance to learn as much as they can.

Janie told me that she'll be going to a *sheltered workshop* next fall for half of each school day. She's excited about that. She'll be earning money and practicing for a full-time job when she graduates, which could be next year if she does okay. She plans to live at home until she's twenty one and then move to a group home downtown. Several people from the workshop live in that home.

Bill probably won't ever get a job. His cerebral palsy is much worse than Marielle's*. Bill has to stay in a wheelchair all the time. When he was born, there was a lot of damage to his brain, so it's very hard for him to control his muscles and it takes him a long time to learn anything. He can only say a few words. He doesn't read or write, but he likes to look at pictures and to play puppets with Patty, one of Ms. Bingham's helpers. Bill's eyes really light up when Patty comes into the room. He can tell when people are friendly and when they care about him.

Janie and Bill are not as smart as the other kids in my school, but they have feelings that are the same as everyone's. Good things make them happy and bad things make them sad or scared. They can tell when people are teasing them, and they don't like it. They want to have friends. You don't have to be around them long to learn that.

Ms. Bingham lets other kids from regular classes help her work

BILL WORKS WITH A THERAPIST.   JANIE OBSERVES CLASSMATES.

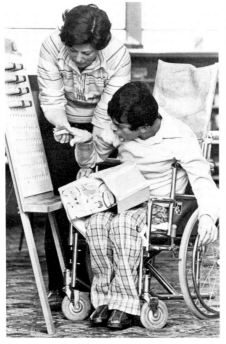

*See Chapter 3—Orthopedic Handicaps

with the kids in the special education room. One day she invited everyone interested to come and ask her questions about mental retardation. We wrote down the questions and answers:

1. *What causes mental retardation?*

Sometimes it's just the way the brain is formed. Sometimes it's caused by damage to the brain. Some retardation is due to lack of proper nutrition while the baby is developing, or lack of opportunity for the baby to learn. Often, the cause is not known.

2. *How can you tell if a person is mentally retarded?*

It isn't always easy to know if a person is mentally retarded unless the condition is a typical one, like Down Syndrome, or is severe. In those cases, the doctor will know as soon as the baby is born. Other kinds of mild retardation will show up as the baby develops more slowly, and walks and talks much later than most other babies. Sometimes retardation isn't noticed until the child starts school. An IQ test may be used, but doing poorly on an IQ test doesn't always mean that a person is retarded.

3. *What is an IQ test?*

It is a test that is designed to measure how much a person can learn. It gives a score for what the person knows, which is called the "mental age," and compares that score with the person's chronological age (how old he or she is). The final score shows how well a person is doing compared to others of the same age. A score of between 90 and 110 is about average. Since there are many reasons why a person might not do well on an IQ test, a low score doesn't always mean much. An IQ test cannot tell you everything about a person's mental abilities.

4. *Why can't an IQ test tell you everything?*

Because it is difficult to separate what a person already knows from what he or she can learn. Some people have had a better chance to learn to use the information the test asks about. Also there are other mental abilities, such as creativity, which are not included in the test. An IQ test doesn't test *all* the mental abilities.

5. *Are mentally retarded persons unpredictable or dangerous?*

No. In fact, studies have shown that mentally retarded persons are *more* predictable and *less* dangerous than the average person.

6. *Is mental retardation like mental illness?*
No.

7. *What is a group home?*

A group home is a place in the community designed for persons with disabilities that make it difficult or dangerous for them to live alone. It is usually a kind of boardinghouse, where the person can

receive whatever help he or she might need with things like budget-
ing money, taking medication, or planning recreation. While the
group home member is an independent adult, supervision is available when it is needed.

8. *How can you be friends with a mentally retarded person?*

That depends on you and on the person. A handicap is not a
reason to make someone your friend, just as it is not a reason to
exclude a person from friendship. Each situation is different. Try to
find something that you have in common or some activity you can
do together. Be patient. Enjoy yourself.

Because of Ms. Bingham and the special education room,
everybody in our school understands what mental retardation is,
and what it is *not*. You know, that makes our school a friendlier
place for *everyone*. I hope we've answered your questions, too. And
I hope I see you around.

CHAPTER FIVE

Learning Disabilities

The term learning disability *refers to certain problems that children of average or above average intelligence can have—problems that make schoolwork difficult and that cannot be solved by regular studying. Sometimes the term* learning handicap *is used instead of* learning disability.

No one really understands what causes learning disabilities, but it is thought that the way in which the nerves and brain cells receive and process information is somewhat different in a learning-disabled person than it is in a normal person. Usually, the problem is one of discrimination. *In this case, discrimination means being able to perceive the differences between things, such as the difference between "n" and "r", or between the sound of "f" and the sound of "sp". Just as people who are color-blind may not be able to discriminate between red and green, the learning-disabled person may not be able to discriminate between certain letters or certain sounds. That makes reading and writing very difficult.*

Whenever a person finds that he or she cannot do what is expected, or what others do with ease, feelings of failure and frustration arise. A learning disabled person must deal with those feelings as well as with the extra work the disability makes necessary.

Our society requires the ability to read and write. Yet many capable persons are limited in those abilities. It is important to discover ways to allow them greater participation in work, in school, and in community life.

My name is Matt Ward.

I'm best known as a water-skier, but people sometimes notice another thing about me. I have a learning disability.

I do a lot of my waterskiing at Lake Isabella. Right now I'm working toward the Sanction Competitions, which are speed-skiing contests.

My whole family races. At one time my Dad broke the world's speed record. He doesn't go out much anymore since his accident,

MATT'S FAVORITE SPORT

so that makes me the most serious skier in the family. Racing is important to me because it's really fun, and it makes up for my having to work so hard at other things—like school.

It's difficult to explain what a learning disability is because it's many different things put together. I'll tell you about it as we go along.

When I race, I'm usually pulled by my friend Denny in his custom-built speedboat. That boat can go from zero to one-hundred miles per hour in ten seconds! My top racing speed is ninety, on a good day.

Speed's exciting, but it's not the whole game. What happens along the way counts, too. I guess you could say the same about school, even though it's a different kind of contest.

Some kids seem to be terrific at schoolwork without even trying. Me, I really work hard just to keep up. I figure it's a job that I do because I have to. I want to be a doctor some day, so I've got to keep on top of it.

They say that the brain is like a complicated computer. If that's so, then my wires are a little crossed up. For instance, I'm right-handed on some things and left-handed on others. And I often get mixed up over which is which.

My memory plays tricks on me, too, and causes two big school problems. One is that I have trouble remembering what letters *sound* like when they're put together. I'm *always* forgetting what happens when "A" and "E" are together. Sometimes the word "neat" seems like it's really two words—"ne at." Sometimes I think it's "net," or "nate," as if it rhymed with "great." And sometimes I can remember that it's "neat." That slows down my reading because I know there wouldn't be a sentence that says, "He was ne at in his work," so I know I have to stop and check it out again.

The other problem is that I can easily forget how a word is supposed to *look*. If I copy it from a book, I get it right. But when

MATT ADJUSTS
HIS LIFE JACKET.

DENNY, HIS BOAT
AND FRIENDS

57

I'm on my own, especially in reading, I sometimes goof up. The word "great" might come out "gneat" because "r" often looks like "n" to me. You'd get stuck, too, if you were trying to read a word like "gneat." I guess I look at the lines too much, and not enough at the spaces. They call that a *perceptual* handicap.

I really felt bad about reading before they discovered that's how I perceive things.

I even write backwards if I'm not careful. Other people have to work hard to do that. For me, it just happens sometimes.

They don't know why my brain turns things around. I'm not slow at understanding, and I can solve hard problems, so I'm not like Sheila, who has a developmental disability. And I can *see*—20:20 vision—so I'm not visually handicapped like Toni. But somehow, after the information gets inside my head, it becomes a little jumbled.

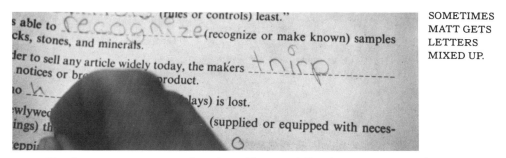

During summer, my brother Jim and I take turns working at our Dad's gas station. That job is easy for me, but there are people with other kinds of learning disabilities who're just as smart as I am but who might have trouble with it. I'm going to exaggerate so you'll get the idea fast. What happens usually isn't this extreme, but since it happens over and over, it adds up to problems.

A HYPERACTIVE KID MIGHT BE ANYWHERE!

One type of learning disability is not being able to sit or stand still. You're all over the place, making everybody nervous. Luckily, most kids outgrow being *hyperactive*.

60

Another problem is having *poor eye-hand coordination*.
This can cause trouble with handwriting and with certain sports. A person with this problem might bang up
the side of a car trying to get the gas nozzle into the
tank. If the car got scratched, the owner would probably
be upset.

WHOOPS! OFF CENTER.

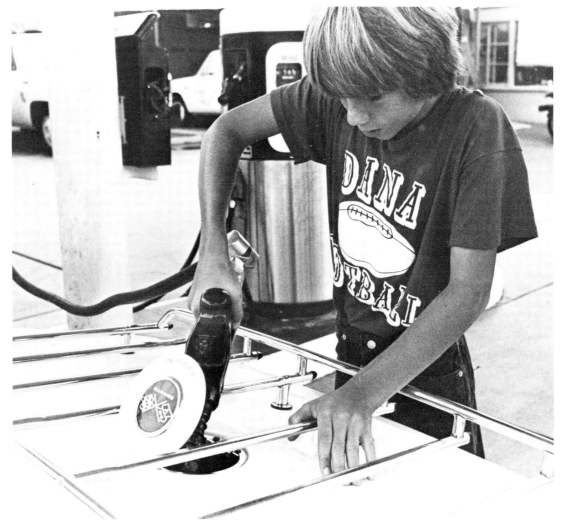

Judging distance can be difficult for some people.
They're not good at putting objects into the right places.
They have a lot of trouble parking cars and they bump
into things, too. You might think they're clumsy, but it's
really a *perceptual handicap*.

Other people have trouble organizing mathematics on paper. If the numbers are not in the proper column, you can't add them up correctly. A person like that wouldn't do well making out a customer's bill. Sometimes this problem is called *dyscalculia*, although it could also be another kind of perceptual handicap.

CHECK THE COLUMNS.

Some people *perseverate*. That means that it's very difficult for them to change from one activity to another. A person who's perseverating might clean a windshield three times and not notice that the customer was getting impatient to leave.

A *VERY* CLEAN WINDSHIELD.

THE RIGHT WORD WON'T COME OUT.

Anomia interferes with a person expressing what's on his or her mind. For example, the attendant *knows* that the car needs a new fan belt but just can't think of the *word* for it. "We've got to change the . . . the . . . um . . . that rubber thing." Anomia happens to everybody once in a while. If it happens a lot, it becomes a learning disability.

Some learning-disabled kids have difficulty with spoken words like the one *I* have with written words. The sound gets *in*, but then it doesn't register right. It's like the time Jim asked me to fill the water bucket, and I thought he said *spill* it! As with other less common learning disabilities, there is no term for that problem.

"FILL? I THOUGH HE SAID *SPILL!*"

You can imagine how annoying it could be to have a handicap like one of those. You *know* you can do the job, but you just get fouled up on certain things. You might start to feel that you're no good . . . a failure. That's the worst part. Nobody should have to feel that way.

When my Mom first noticed *I* was having trouble, she took me to a child development clinic to see what was going on. They gave me a lot of tests, physical and mental, and they told us that there's at least one person in almost every classroom who has some kind of learning disability. Often you can barely notice it. My problem is pretty common. In fact, so common that many schools have special materials and special programs to help kids like me. They teach us to focus on the details that give us trouble. Sometimes the doctor will prescribe a special diet or medication, since it's really a *physical* problem. And the teacher may even change the way she tests so that the student has a better chance to show what he or she understands.

So now I'm in a special program. I don't know how long I'll need to stay there. That depends on how I do. I've learned to correct many of my usual mistakes myself, though I still like a little help now and then.

My friend JP helps me, too. Doing our homework together improves my concentration so that I don't get bored and let my mind wander.

Of course, not all learning problems are learning disabilities. If you miss a lot of school, you'll get behind. If you don't pay attention in class, you'll miss information that you need. If the language you speak at school is different from the one you use at home, you might get confused. However, those things are not learning disabilities. They are not a result of something not working quite right in your brain.

I think the worst part of my learning disability is that I get

SOME DAYS ARE HARD
AND DISCOURAGING.

awfully tired of goofing up and looking like a failure. Even though I understand what my problem is, it's hard. And it's embarrassing because I get upset easily, "frustrated," my Dad says. I wish I didn't. I get so angry at myself sometimes that I feel like crying. When that happens, I try to get away alone for a while.

Jim's a "normie" . . . he doesn't have any kind of disability, so far as I can tell. He says he sometimes wishes he had mine, so he'd have an excuse when he makes mistakes. That's one thing I'd catch it for from my folks—making phoney excuses.

My Dad says that if I really try, no matter how it turns out, that's good enough. In that respect there's no such thing as failure.

I don't have to be perfect, but when it comes to school, I have to give it my best shot. It's the only way to go.

CHAPTER SIX

Behavior Disorders

What makes people behave the way they do? What are emotions? How do we learn to understand our feelings? How do we control our behavior? People have asked these questions throughout history. They are questions that we are still unable to answer completely.

Growing up is a process of learning about oneself and about others, about how to relate the unique individual that one is to the demands of the surrounding world. For a healthy person it is a process that doesn't end with adulthood, but continues throughout the entire life. It is a process that is difficult at times, and has, for most people, many ups and downs.

In this chapter you will meet three children whose feelings are causing them personal unhappiness. Two of them are also getting into trouble with others at home and at school.

These three stories—of Ken, Laura, and John—are typical of what sometimes happens to a person's feelings and behavior. But no two individuals are exactly alike. No two problems are exactly alike. That's why there are no easy answers.

Each emotional and behavioral problem has to be worked out individually. One way to begin is to try to understand what kinds of feelings are involved in the problem and what situations arouse those feelings.

Ken

Ken was worried again. Not the usual bad worried feeling that he had most of the time. Not the funny feeling he sometimes got that lasted for days and made everything seem unreal and far away. This time it was worse. It was like both of those feelings at once, and it was scary—as if something terrible would happen any minute.

Sitting at the painting table with Phil and Moises, it seemed to nine-year-old Ken as if his friends had suddenly become total strangers.

What were they laughing about? Why were they painting those squares and circles? Painting was stupid! Nobody should be painting. Didn't they know how stupid it was? They shouldn't just sit there and laugh and paint when everything was so awful and scary and far away.

Then Ken got an idea. If he took the red paint and threw it all over Phil's paper, that would stop the painting and the laughing and maybe it would stop the awful thing that was going to happen. All that red paint might just cover up everything and make it stop.

Ken grabbed the paint and threw, but in the very moment that the paint hit Phil's paper and Phil shouted, "Hey, what're you doing?" Ken knew that it hadn't worked. Nothing had changed

KEN THREW THE PAINT.

except that now the whole class was a sea of strangers staring at him, pushing him farther and farther away.

Without realizing what he was doing, Ken bolted across the room and out the back door to his special place by the fence. The iron wires felt comforting between his fingers as he began to cry.

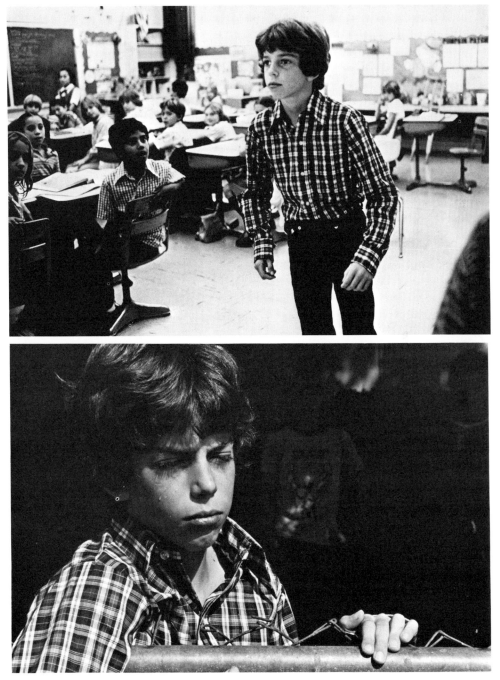

Laura

Thirteen-year-old Laura knew that the "Big Three" were talking about her again. She could see them out of the corner of her eye, there in the back of the class where they always sat together third period. Just because they were the most popular and the best students didn't give them the right to put anybody else down. But that's what they did, and it was Laura they usually did it to.

The whole thing was so unfair. Every time Laura started to feel comfortable enough to start to make friends, her father's job made it necessary for her family to move again. Now here she was in southern California where everybody acted so cool, and you were some kind of idiot if you didn't know the very latest thing to do or say or wear. She had no idea how to get along with these kids. They had everything sewn up from the beginning. You would have had to have been *born* here to make friends with them.

Laura sank a little farther into her chair. It was no use. She felt ugly and stupid and beaten. She decided that she would ignore everyone and pretend she wasn't there. Maybe she just wasn't meant to have friends. She would teach herself not to expect anything that she formerly wanted. Things would be different when she grew up. She'd try to wait until then.

THE "BIG THREE." LAURA IS SURE THEY ARE TALKING ABOUT HER.

SHE FEELS LEFT OUT AGAIN.

John

John was angry. He was looking for someone who dared to cross him. He'd show them. He'd show anyone who thought they could push him around.

If he could get away with it again, he'd ditch school, but he knew that one more time would get him expelled and he hadn't figured out what to do then. John had seen more than a few guys, including his older brother and several of his friends, genuinely wasted because they couldn't finish school. He didn't know what finishing school really accomplished, but he knew he didn't want to have to scrounge the way they did.

As he sat in Ms. Wilkins's fourth-period English, John felt his resentment rising. No doubt Ms. Wilkins would be on his back again today. She hated the sight of him. All that stuff about prepositions and public speaking had nothing to do with him, and he had made that very clear to her.

Things had been quiet at home for a while. Then Dad had come back again and the late nights, the fights, and the beatings had begun all over. John felt the bruise on his arm where Dad had socked him this morning for accidentally spilling coffee. It made John furious that Mom let Dad get away with acting as he did.

JOHN'S MIND IS NOT ON HIS SCHOOL WORK.

When Dad was around, she just seemed to crumble. Yeah, Dad was about the only person John knew who got what he wanted. Because he took it, John thought, *because he took it*.

Ignoring Ms. Wilkins's voice from the front of the class, John started teasing Steve about his hair. He liked to get a rise out of Steve, who always looked as if he had been dressed by a maid and a butler. Not much bothered Steve, so it often took a while before John could get the reaction he wanted.

"John, take your seat, please," came Ms. Wilkins's voice. John brushed off the interruption as if it were a fly. "Oh, Stevie. Who does you hair? Here, let me rearrange a few curls for you." John ran his hand backwards along the top of Steve's head.

"John, I said I want you to take your seat."

JOHN TEASES STEVE. THE TEASING GETS ABUSIVE.

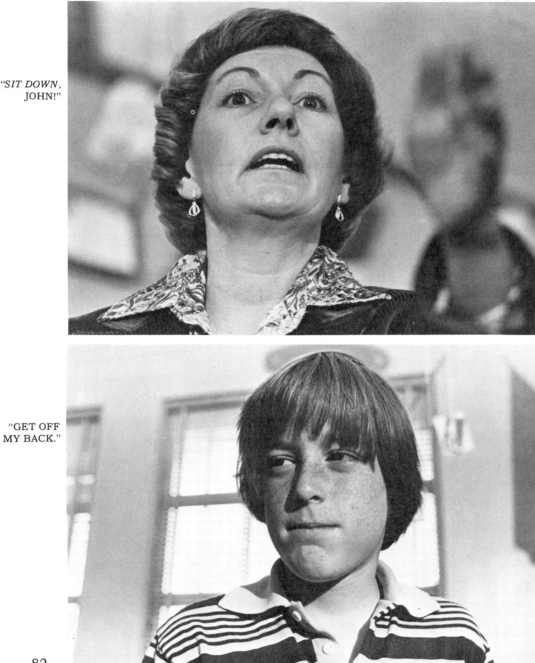

"*SIT DOWN*, JOHN!"

"GET OFF MY BACK."

"Where should I take it, Ms. Wilkins?" A good reply. A nice TV-type comeback. Everyone was laughing. Except Ms. Wilkins, of course.

"SIT DOWN, JOHN!"

"Get off my back, Ms. Wilkins, you jerk!" That did it. Now he'd be sent to the office. Well, at least that meant no more prepositions for a while.

Mr. Felton

Three different kids. Three different problems. Yet their problems all have one thing in common—feelings.

As a school principal, I see a lot of different kids. No two are alike. It's part of my job to help kids handle their problems.

Most kids think that being sent to the office is strictly punishment, but that's not true. Of course, we have rules at school that must be followed in order to make things run smoothly for everyone. If a student doesn't follow the rules, he or she is making things hard for others. When someone is sent to my office, I try to find out what's bothering that person or what's making it difficult for him or her to behave well.

The day that John came in to see me went something like this:

"He hit me again this morning, Mr. Felton. He socked me real hard. Then he left. But I'll have to see him again tonight. He makes me so mad! That's no way for a Dad to act, is it?"

"Well, John, you can't treat other people the way your Dad treats you. That'll only make things worse. But I know how you feel. You'd like to hit someone, too, since

you know you can't hit your Dad. I don't blame you for that.

"You know, one thing you might do to work off some of those feelings is to spend some time in the gym. Really use those muscles. See if that doesn't help you feel better. And I'd like the counselor to talk to you and your mother. Maybe the three of you can work out something that will make things easier for you at home."

"Not my Mom. She's too busy. She'd be mad. Couldn't I just talk to you?"

"OK. I've got some time. . . ."

86   John's going to make it. Between the two of us, we'll help him

find a way to make school a good experience, and home less of a problem.

I can help John because he was willing to level with me about what he really thinks and feels, and about what's happening to him.

It's not always easy to find out what's bothering a child. Sometimes the child doesn't know. However, certain situations turn up again and again for kids who are troubled.

For instance, having to move frequently can be tough. Leaving old friends is sad, and it's not always easy to make new ones.

Another situation that often causes pain happens when parents don't get along. It's frightening to listen to and watch parents fight. Divorce can be upsetting, too. Sometimes children think that they are to blame for the divorce, which is rarely true.

Sometimes things feel very unfair, such as Mom or Dad never being home, or not having enough money for food or nice clothes.

Getting behind in schoolwork is another kind of problem—one that can have many different causes. Once someone gets behind, he or she will feel very frustrated, regardless of the reason for getting behind. Then, there are two problems to solve—catching up, plus whatever caused the falling behind in the first place.

Nobody likes to be frustrated or afraid. No one likes to feel hurt or rejected. But sometimes things can make individuals so upset that their behavior creates real problems. When a child's behavior causes trouble often, we sometimes say that the child is *emotionally disturbed* or has a *behavior disorder*.

Many things can contribute to emotional disturbance. Some are complicated and require the professional help of a psychologist, psychiatrist, or doctor. Ken, for example, doesn't know why he feels so afraid and so angry even when nothing *seems* to be wrong. It could be that there is some imbalance in the chemistry of his body. Since we don't know the answer, we try to help him by being understanding.

LAURA ABOUT TO MAKE A POOR DECISION

It doesn't always take an expert to know the difference between a person who is very upset and one who is simply not behaving as well as he or she could. But sometimes it's hard to tell. That's where a teacher, counselor, or principal can help.

Laura was just about to make a bad decision when her teacher, Ms. Harris, saw what was happening. Ms. Harris had a talk with the "Big Three" and pointed out how a little help from them might get Laura accepted by the class. She reminded them of how it feels to be in a new place where everyone is a stranger. Once they set out to get to know Laura, it was pretty easy to make friends. And Laura didn't have to decide to be unfriendly and alone. Changing that decision might have helped prevent Laura from becoming emotionally disturbed!

IT HELPS TO
TALK THINGS OUT.

NOT SO ALONE NOW

89

Everybody's got *some* problems. Having problems is nothing to be ashamed of. In fact, how can a person solve a problem without first admitting that there is one?

If you're feeling bad, it helps to have someone to talk to—someone who can help you figure out what to do. This person can be a parent, teacher, principal, counselor, psychologist, doctor, or even a friend. And if you see someone who seems to be having a hard time, why not see if *you* can help?

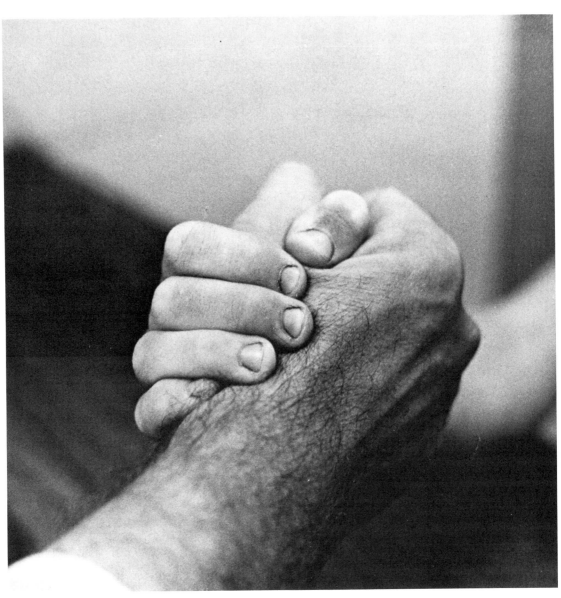

FRIENDS!

Glossary

ADL	*Activities of Daily Living.* Includes the various aspects of feeding and dressing, personal grooming, getting around in the home and community, etc.
Ameslan	*American Sign Language.* One of several sign languages used by hearing- and/or speech-impaired persons.
Amputation	Surgical removal of a limb or part of a limb.
Anomia	A type of expressive aphasia characterized by difficulty in recalling words or names of objects.
Aphasia	An impairment of the ability to use or understand oral language due to neurological damage to areas of the brain associated with language function. May result in inability to understand language (receptive aphasia), inability to express oneself in language (expressive aphasia), or both. Aphasia is not a disease.
Architectural Barrier	Any physical aspect of the community that prevents a person from full, safe participation. For example, stairs are an architectural barrier for a person in a wheelchair.

Autism	A severe disturbance of mental and emotional development in children. Autistic youngsters are extremely withdrawn and show little or no interest in other people or in the usual activities of childhood.
Behavior Disorder	A persistent inability to conform to the rules and/or expectations of the normal environment.
Blind	A general term that covers a range of visual impairments. Requires special adjustment beyond glasses or contact lenses.
Braille	A system of reading and writing that uses raised dots to represent letters.
Braillewriter	A machine similar to a typewriter used for making Braille characters.
Cerebral Palsy	Any one or a combination of conditions in which movement is impaired due to brain damage. May or may not be accompanied by *mental retardation*.
Deaf	A general term that covers a range of hearing loss. Usually requires special adjustment in order to communicate.
Developmental Disability	A condition that occurs before birth or during the first twelve years of life and that will continue to handicap the person for the rest of his or her life. Cerebral palsy, Down Syndrome, epilepsy, and mental retardation are examples of developmental disabilities.
Disability	Any physical or mental condition that causes a person to be unable to do something he or she could otherwise do.
Down Syndrome	A developmental disability usually characterized by lowered intellectual ability; slanted folds of the eyelids; large tongue; broad, flat bridge of the nose; and poor muscle tone. Is considered to account for the largest number of retarded persons where the cause of retardation is known.

Emotionally Disturbed	A broad term referring to chronic constant or periodic feelings which are extremely uncomfortable to the individual and/or others in the environment. May result in inappropriate or destructive behavior.
Epilepsy	A chronic disorder of the brain characterized by recurring attacks of unconsciousness and/or convulsions. Most types of epilepsy can be controlled with medication.
EMR	Educable Mentally Retarded. Mildly retarded persons who can complete high school and become employed when given extra help and certain special classes. Their IQ usually measures about 50 to 69 points.
Finger-Spelling	Using the position of the hands and fingers to represent letters of the alphabet. (See diagram, Page 18.)
Group Home	A type of boardinghouse designed to meet the needs of handicapped persons. Usually specializes in one major type of disability, such as physical, mental, or emotional disorders.
Handicap	The degree to which an individual has difficulty performing in a given situation.
Impairment	An actual physical defect that results in less than average functioning of the impaired and/or related part or parts. It may or may not lead to a *disability*.
Learning Disability	One or more problems that children of average or above-average intelligence may have with schoolwork. Cannot be remedied by regular studying or tutoring. May be the result of neurological differences or disorders, allergies, or other unknown causes.
Legg-Perthes Disease	A disease of the femur characterized by loss of bone tissue at the joint where the femur meets the pelvis. The tissue will regenerate, but pressure must be kept off the bone during this phase so that

the bone will resume a normal rounded shape and not be flattened by contact with the pelvis. Usually occurs in boys aged six to ten and runs a three-year course.

Listening Training	Special training in the discrimination of speech sounds that helps the hearing-impaired person make maximum use of whatever hearing he or she may have. Sometimes called *auditory training*.
Mental Retardation	An impairment of the mental processes that slows and limits general intellectual functioning (the ability to learn) *and* that reduces the individual's capacity for personal independence and social maturity.
Mobility Training	The training that visually impaired persons receive from professionals in getting around the environment. Includes the use of the white cane or dog guide, the body protective technique, orientation, use of auditory and tactile clues, memorization of routes, etc.
Normie	Slang term referring to a non-handicapped person.
Orientation	A series of techniques that, when mastered, allow the visually impaired person to understand where he or she *is* within the environment. An important part of learning to travel independently.
Orthopedic	Involving the skeletal system (i.e., the bones).
Paralysis	Partial or complete loss of voluntary movement in some part or all of the body as a result of injury to the nervous system, brain, or muscular mechanism. May be accompanied by loss of sensation in the affected part(s).
Perceptual Handicap	A broad term referring to learning disabilities that are due to problems in interpreting the meaning of the information received by the senses. Is thought to have a neurological basis.
Peroneal Muscular Atrophy	A disease of the peroneal nerve that causes the muscles, especially those of the legs, to fail to grow.

Perseverate	A tendency to continue an activity once it has been started and to be unable to change or stop the activity even though it is no longer appropriate.
PMR	Profoundly Mentally Retarded (sometimes called Severely Mentally Retarded). Mentally retarded persons whose disability is so severe that they require special care and do not attend regular school. They may always need help with activities of daily living, often because of additional physical problems. Their IQ usually measures below 40 points.
Sheltered Workshop	A special employment situation designed for persons whose disabilities prevent them from participating in regular competitive jobs. Allows the person to work at his or her own pace.
Signing	Communicating by using the hands, fingers, and gestures to represent words or concepts.
Stuttering	Speaking with breaks or repetitions of words or parts of words.
TMR	Trainable Mentally Retarded. Moderately retarded persons who usually can be trained to care for themselves independently and to work at specially designed jobs such as those in sheltered workshops. Their IQ usually measures about 40 to 54 points.
Visually Impaired	Having a physical defect involving the reception or transmission of visual images.
VH	Visually handicapped. Visual impairment that requires some form of special adjustment beyond glasses or contact lenses.